DISCARD

For Mediik'm Gyamkx (Neil J. Sterrit). A Gitxsan warrior who endeavoured to preserve our existence. His support for our Wilp and encouragement to me has always been invaluable.

— H.G. / B.D.H.


For Elkin, who lights up every room: may your life be full of magical stories. It's a privilege and a joy to be your auntie.
— N.D.

# THE FROG MOTHER

By Hetxw'ms Gyetxw (Brett D. Huson)

Illustrated by Natasha Donovan

HIGHWATER
PRESS

# Starting Together

This is the time of Lasa ya'a, the Spring Salmon's Returning Home Moon. The sun crests the mountain in the east, casting rays of light through the trees toward a small pond that is full of life. Nox Ga'naaw, the frog mother, has spawned[1] a mass of 500 eggs that float freely among the aquatic[2] plants.

[1] **Spawn** means to release a large number of eggs.

[2] **Aquatic** plants and animals live in water.

This time of birth for Nox Ga'naaw is also a sacred time for the Gitxsan. Lasa ya'a symbolizes a renewal of the land. It marks the return of the spring salmon and a change in season. The Gitxsan revere[1] the frog as the storyteller. It's with the tongue that people communicate. Because of this, Gitxsan stories and songs say that the frog's long tongue allows it to speak all languages and truths of the universe.[2] As nightfall arrives, these primarily nocturnal[3] creatures share their evening stories and songs.

Four days after Nox Ga'naaw placed her eggs into the pond, they stir and begin to hatch. The little frog larvae,[1] called tadpoles, leave their eggs and swim out into the pond. These small black larvae have yet to change into their frog-shaped bodies, so they depend on their tails to propel[2] them around their environment to find food. Like the Gitxsan, the tadpoles are omnivorous, eating both plants and animals.

[1] **Larvae** are the young form of an animal that transforms into an adult through metamorphosis.
[2] **Propel** means to push or drive forward.

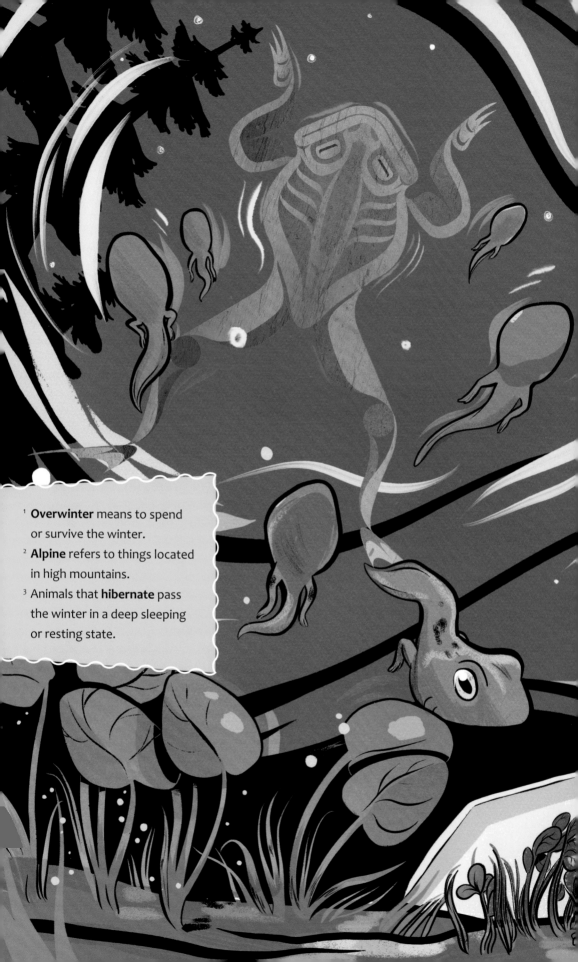

¹ **Overwinter** means to spend or survive the winter.
² **Alpine** refers to things located in high mountains.
³ Animals that **hibernate** pass the winter in a deep sleeping or resting state.

The young tadpoles spend the summer feeding and working hard to sprout their legs, giving them the shape of their frog mother. When Lasa gwineekxw, the Getting-Used-to-Cold Moon arrives, they will overwinter[1] in the unfrozen depths of this alpine[2] pond. The tadpoles and small frogs will settle themselves into the mud bottoms, where they will hibernate[3] until spring.

# Growing Together

It is June, Lasa maa'y, the Gathering and Preparing Berries Moon. The tadpoles have grown into their juvenile[1] shapes. They now look like Nox Ga'naaw. Some have migrated[2] to other nearby waterways, ponds, and lakes, but a young female has chosen to stay in the pond where she was born. However, staying here means she must avoid a hungry lelt. Lelt is how the Gitxsan say snake.

[1] A **juvenile** animal is not yet fully grown.
[2] **Migrate** means to move from one region or habitat to another.

¹ **Vegetation** refers to the plants or plant cover in a particular habitat.

This pond is full of the insects and vegetation¹ the juvenile female loves to eat. Her favourite meal is kw'aat'ax, the slug. She is growing fast, and like the other female frogs in the pond, she has quickly outgrown the males.

Not far from her home, Gitxsan children spend their days exploring their surroundings at a berry-picking camp. Because of their reverence for Ga'naaw, some children have thrown maa'y, berries, into the water. Not to turn down a free meal, the frogs gladly gobble up these gifts.

# Becoming the Mother

Five years have passed, and Lasa ya'a has returned once again. The young female frog has become Nox Ga'naaw, the frog mother. Her body has transformed and matured[1] to carry the beautiful life and future of her species. Almost too quiet to hear, the smaller male frogs sing songs of birth and renewal. Nox Ga'naaw is aware of the changes in her body. She makes her way to a bed of growing algae[2] and vegetation that appeals to her needs.

[1] An animal that has **matured** is fully grown or developed.

[2] **Algae** are simple organisms that live mainly in water and make their food through photosynthesis.

Nox Ga'naaw has continued the cycle of her family, a cycle that has existed for over 200 million years. Many of the other frogs have been, and will be, a source of food for other species in their ecosystem.[1] As the Gitxsan have borne witness since time immemorial,[2] there is a delicate balance of food for all living in their realm. Nox Ga'naaw and her offspring are an integral piece of this balance that is life.

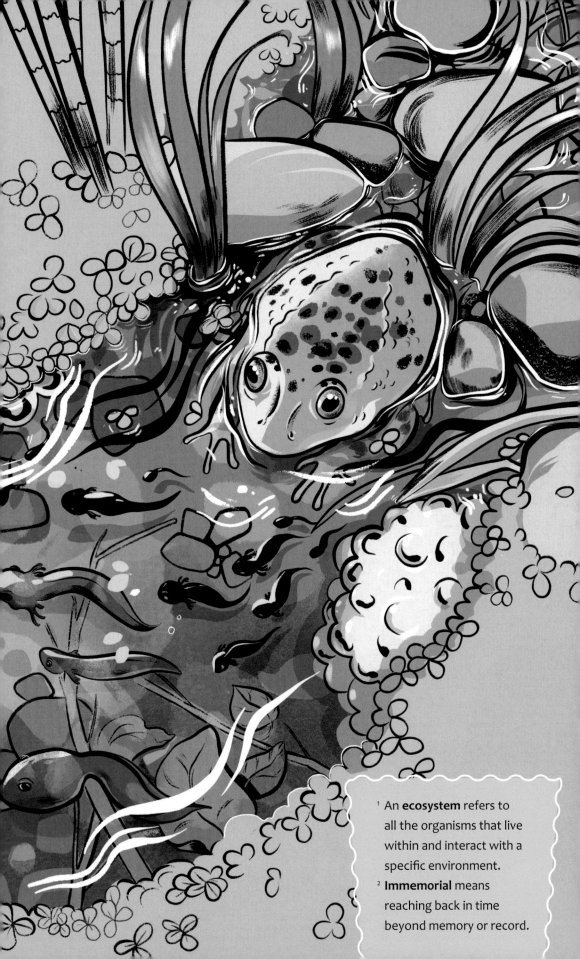

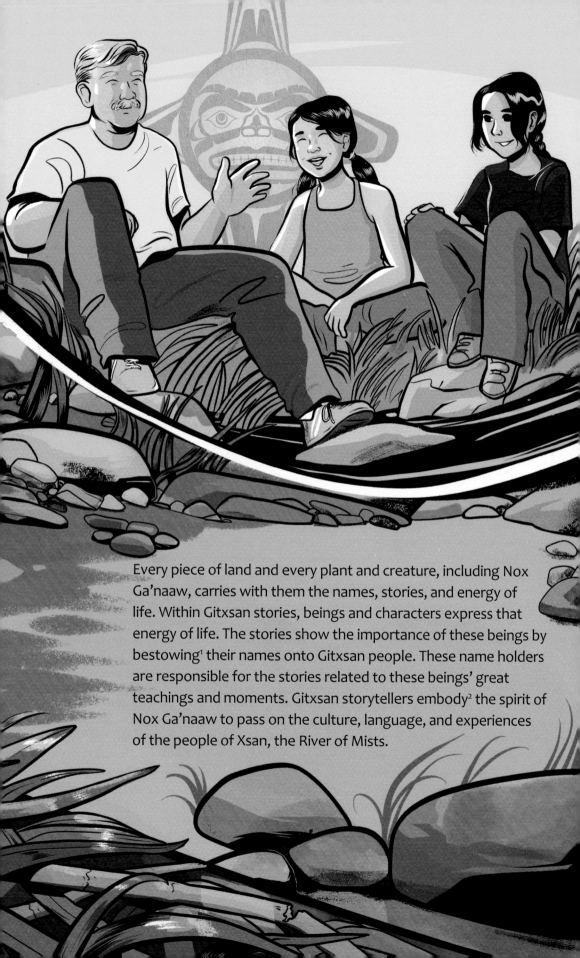

Every piece of land and every plant and creature, including Nox Ga'naaw, carries with them the names, stories, and energy of life. Within Gitxsan stories, beings and characters express that energy of life. The stories show the importance of these beings by bestowing[1] their names onto Gitxsan people. These name holders are responsible for the stories related to these beings' great teachings and moments. Gitxsan storytellers embody[2] the spirit of Nox Ga'naaw to pass on the culture, language, and experiences of the people of Xsan, the River of Mists.

# The Gitxsan

The Gitxsan Nation are Indigenous peoples from unceded territories in the Northwest Interior of British Columbia. These 35,000 square kilometres of land cradle the headwaters of Xsan or "the River of Mists," also known by its colonial name, the Skeena River. The land defines who the Gitxsan people are.

The Nation follows a matrilineal line, and all rights, privileges, names, and stories come from the mothers. Lax Seel (Frog), Lax Gibuu (Wolf), Lax Skiik (Eagle), and Gisghaast (Fireweed) are the four clans of the people. It is taboo to marry a fellow clan member, even when there are no blood ties.

The four clans are divided among the territories by way of the Wilp system. A Wilp, or "house group," is a group comprising one or more families. Each Wilp has a Head Chief and Wing Chiefs, who are guided by Elders and members of their Wilp. Currently, there are 62 house groups, and each governs their portion of the Gitxsan Territories.

# The Gitxsan Moons

| K'uholxs | Stories and Feasting Moon | January |
| Lasa hu'mal | Cracking Cottonwood and Opening Trails Moon | February |
| Wihlaxs | Black Bear's Walking Moon | March |
| Lasa ya'a | Spring Salmon's Returning Home Moon | April |
| Lasa 'yanja | Budding Trees and Blooming Flowers Moon | May |
| Lasa maa'y | Gathering and Preparing Berries Moon | June |
| Lasa 'wiihun | Fisherman's Moon | July |
| Lasa lik'i'nxsw | Grizzly Bear's Moon | August |
| Lasa gangwiikw | Groundhog Hunting Moon | September |
| Lasa xsin laaxw | Catching-Lots-of-Trout Moon | October |
| Lasa gwineekxw | Getting-Used-to-Cold Moon | November |
| Lasa 'wiigwineekxw or Lasa gunkw' ats | Severe Snowstorms and Sharp Cold Moon | December |
| Ax wa | Shaman's Moon | A blue moon, which is a second full moon in a single month |

Kispiox
River

Stekyodin

Bulkley
River

Skeena River

**Canada Council** **Conseil des Arts**
**for the Arts** **du Canada**

We acknowledge the support of the Canada Council for the Arts.
Nous remercions le Conseil des arts du Canada de son soutien.

HighWater Press gratefully acknowledges the financial support of the Province of Manitoba through the Department of Sport, Culture and Heritage and the Manitoba Book Publishing Tax Credit, and the Government of Canada through the Canada Book Fund (CBF), for our publishing activities.

HighWater Press is an imprint of Portage & Main Press.
Printed and bound in Canada by Friesens
Design by Relish New Brand Experience
Cover Art by Natasha Donovan

**Library and Archives Canada Cataloguing in Publication**

Title: The frog mother / by Hetxw'ms Gyetxw (Brett D. Huson) ; illustrated by Natasha Donovan.
Names: Huson, Brett D., author. | Donovan, Natasha, illustrator.
Series: Huson, Brett D., Mothers of Xsan.
Description: Series statement: Mothers of Xsan
Identifiers: Canadiana (print) 20200367412 | Canadiana (ebook) 20200367447 | ISBN 9781553799016 (hardcover) | ISBN 9781553799023 (EPUB) | ISBN 9781553799030 (PDF)
Subjects: LCSH: Columbia spotted frog—Life cycles—Juvenile literature. | LCSH: Columbia spotted frog—British Columbia—Juvenile literature. | LCSH: Indigenous peoples—British Columbia—Juvenile literature. | LCGFT: Picture books.
Classification: LCC QL668.E27 H87 2021 | DDC j597.8/92—dc23

24 23 22 21        1 2 3 4 5

 HIGHWATER
PRESS

www.highwaterpress.com
Winnipeg, Manitoba
Treaty 1 Territory and homeland of the Métis Nation